Leaves of Life

Creating Therapy Gardens for People with Disabilities

ESTHER DEANS

ANGUS
& ROBERTSON

An imprint of HarperCollins*Publishers*

This book is dedicated to the 'handicapable', those wonderful people who have overcome their disabilities.

AN ANGUS & ROBERTSON BOOK
An imprint of HarperCollinsPublishers

First published in Australia in 1991 by
CollinsAngus&Robertson Publishers Pty Limited (ACN 009 913 517)
A division of HarperCollinsPublishers (Australia) Pty Limited
Unit 4, Eden Park, 31 Waterloo Road, North Ryde
NSW 2113, Australia

William Collins Publishers Ltd
31 View Road, Glenfield, Auckland 10, New Zealand

Angus & Robertson (UK)
77-85 Fulham Palace Road, London W6 8JB, United Kingdom

National Library of Australia
Cataloguing-in-Publication data:

Deans, Esther.
  Leaves of Life

  Includes Index

  ISBN 0 207 17062 2

  1. Gardening — Therapeutic use. 2. Gardening
  for the handicapped. i. Title

635

Cover photo by David Young
Printed in the People's Republic of China

5 4 3 2 1
95 94 93 92 91

Contents

ACKNOWLEDGEMENTS

Thanks to the numerous people who have contributed to the writing of this special book—to the therapists who have used the No Dig method of gardening to assist people with problems to experience the healing touch of mother earth.

My special thanks to my husband Tom for his constant help, endless typing and understanding, and thanks also to friends who have supplied photographs (all other photographs by David Young).

My appreciation and grateful thanks go to John Miller, who inspired me to write my first two books—*Esther Deans' Gardening Book: growing without digging* and *Esther Deans' Cookbook: garden to kitchen*—and for his confidence and encouragement to me to write this third book.

❖ ❖ ❖

For those interested in contacting other garden enthusiasts, why not contact

Australian Horticultural Correspondence School
264 Swansea Road
Lillydale Victoria 3140
Phone: (03) 736 1882
Contact: John Mason

What a wonderful inspiration John Mason of Victoria had to start a correspondence school for gardeners. It has meant so much to many people, especially those with a disability, to be able to have contact with others.

❖ ❖ ❖

F O R E W O R D

Every garden lover knows the therapeutic value of gardening. Fortunately the rest of the world is now discovering it and gardening is being used to calm and/or interest people who were disturbed or lacked an interest through illness, disability, or other problems.

A few years ago American research proved (if it needs proving!) that gardening is good for you. The National Heart Foundation supports this view with a rose called Young-at-Heart, which is their reminder to all that gardening is good for the heart. The 'Life Be In It' programme advocates gardening as a means of keeping healthy. Throughout the country horticultural therapy associations and schools are being formed to cater for the specialised needs of the elderly and physically or mentally disabled people.

Esther Deans' concept of the No Dig Garden is tailor-made for these groups and, as well, has a wide appeal because it saves time and effort and is friendly to the environment since it keeps the soil in good repair.

It is logical to take the concept a step further by stressing the healing qualities of gardening. Esther Deans recognises that everyone, whatever their state of health, will find therapeutic benefit in gardening. This book sets out to prove that point and to introduce us to a happier life style through the garden.

VALERIE SWANE, O.B.E.
DURAL
20 January, 1991

ESTHER DEANS' STORY

When I was a child, I remember how much I enjoyed being rewarded for a job well done. I remember receiving a pat on the back with a hearty 'good girl', or that little gift left to be discovered on the bed—surprise, surprise—for doing well in exams, or the promise of a special treat for giving a helping hand when needed.

Yes, I remember, and looking back now and in the years to come I will say 'thanks for the memories', for the many wonderful experiences, for the thousands of people young and old, from all walks of life, who have shared this time with me. I will also be thankful for the opportunity to visit many places, for the hundreds of folk I have not yet met but with whom I have corresponded and for the tremendous interest and support from the media. Above all thanks a thousand times to the good Lord who prepared and guided me in all I have done.

Life is exciting and there is much to do. It is beholden to every right thinking person to see that our children learn to love our beautiful world: to understand the wonders of creation, the soil, the water, the sun and moon, the rainbow, the magic of the wind and the rolling sea; to understand the miracle of their own bodies, their needs and how to keep healthy and happy.

Back in 1977 on an open garden day, Jan and John Miller came to meet a dear friend in my garden. Their friend felt the garden would give her something fresh to think about as her son had recently died. John was a scout for Rigby's, the publishers, and two weeks later he rang up to invite me to write a book about my backyard garden. He asked me to write just as I talked to the people visiting my garden. What a surprise! I had answered many letters and written articles, but I had never written a book.

John suggested I write the first chapter and supply headings for the following chapters. The family said 'Give it a go, Mum'. A challenge is always exciting, so I decided to 'give it a go'. For two whole weeks it was sheer agony waiting for inspiration and trying to make a start. On a Tuesday night, exactly two weeks later, I decided it was to be that night or never. By 11 p.m. there was still no mark on the paper; at 1.45 a.m. I put my pen down. It was no use, I did not know how to start to write a book. With a feeling of agitation I went to the kitchen to make myself a hot drink, but before I got there the inspiration came as I thought: 'Why do we want to have a garden?' That was it! I went back to write down the heading, and my pen did not stop until 3.30 a.m.—words just flowed on and on. I was truly guided.

Subsequent headings were not difficult: garden making, herbs, seeds, creatures in the garden, planting time etc. The photographs to be used in this book had been taken by my family over the years, and they added to the simple backyard garden idea.

John was delighted, but Rigby's rejected it, which turned out to be the best thing that could have happened. John took the book to Harper and Row and it became the first book they published in Australia.

By November 1977, the *Esther Deans' Gardening Book: Growing Without Digging* had been printed. When Mr Watson, manager of Harper and Row, presented me with the first book off the press he said: 'What better way to put our grass roots down than [with] a little garden book.'

I decided to give two thirds of my royalties for the book to the spastic children who could not run on the soft warm earth, and to the blind children who could not see the wonder of all creation.

On Sunday, 13 November 1977, my book was dedicated to service and the next day it was launched at St Ives shopping centre. It was a very simple, friendly gathering hosted by the local bookshop and I shared the occasion with relatives, friends and shoppers. By the end of the day, 317 books had been autographed. By the end of December 1977 two more printings, each of 5000, were made. Little did I imagine that by October 1990 82,500 copies of that little book would have been printed.

It was a very exciting time following the launch, with book signing promotions, giving talks and showing many visitors my garden. I was also honoured by Sir Garfield Barwick, who presented me with a certificate awarding me Life Membership of The Royal New South Wales Institution for Deaf and Blind Children.

After the success of the gardening book, I was asked in 1978 to write another book, *Esther Deans' Garden Cook Book—from garden to kitchen*. I enjoy preparing vegetables for our family meals and making up new recipes, so this book was not as much of a problem to begin as the gardening book had been. Once again, Harper and Row were the publishers and it was publicly launched at St Ives Shopping Centre. The royalties from the 12,500 copies printed were shared with the Multiple Sclerosis Society and the Lorna Hodgkinson Sunshine Home, plus others who needed help.

It was requested that both books be transcribed into braille by Miss Betty Burr of Brisbane. I had no idea this was happening until I was invited to a meeting at the Queensland Braille Writing Association at Annerley, Queensland, to receive copies. I was completely overwhelmed. Since that day many copies in braille have been sent to other countries, and to various schools and individuals as gifts. It was being printed by the Braille Press in Edinburgh when I was there in 1981, and a copy was sent to St Johns, Newfoundland.

There was also a request from a young man in Brisbane who was visually impaired, to have my books recorded on cassette. Many recorded copies have been made since then—and sent as far away as Kenya—and in Sydney tapes were made for the Print Handicapped Library.

Interviews for television, radio, magazines and newspapers; invitations to speak about the No Dig garden throughout the country—in Sydney, Perth, Adelaide and Melbourne—and in New Zealand, all helped to spread the message to people who wanted to have gardens without digging. Many exciting and wonderful stories could be told about gardens made at various schools and centres for people with handicaps; about gardens made on table tops, on old beds, on rock, hard clay and sand; of gardens made on old carpet, on old coats from a shearing shed, on concrete under a clothes hoist, as well as on black oily soil in Houston, Texas. People in all walks of life have enjoyed making gardens without digging.

Because I no longer live in St Ives and have my beautiful vegetable garden, I can look back and appreciate how the years of working in the garden helped restore my health—and give thanks for all the wonderful things that happened during those years. Now I can say 'thanks for the memories' and thanks again for the opportunity to create different gardens in the retirement village where I now live. Gardens in the Nursing Centre, where the elderly residents can enjoy the flowers and their fragrances, are referred to as 'Esther's Therapy Gardens'—this is quite exciting.

How humble and privileged all this has made me feel, and I ask why the good Lord chose me, a little backyard gardener, to be able to help so many people.

My garden in the late 1960s, before the No Dig garden—there is no goodness in the soil.

Here you can see the first effects of the No Dig garden, in the early 1970s.

MAKING A NO DIG GARDEN

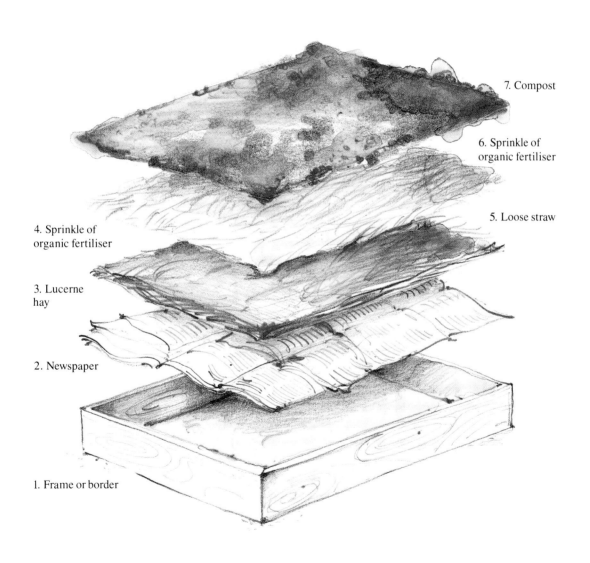

7. Compost

6. Sprinkle of
organic fertiliser

5. Loose straw

4. Sprinkle of
organic fertiliser

3. Lucerne
hay

2. Newspaper

1. Frame or border

I am writing this book especially for those people with disabilities which usually stop them having a garden of their own. It is for those who would like to watch a tiny seed grow into a beautiful plant, and for those who would like to be able to feel the earth with hands or feet. But sight is not necessary when one can smell the soft perfume of the tiny violet, the wondrous fragrance of a velvety soft rose, or feel the varied texture of the many plants and trees that grow from our soil.

The following photos will, I am sure, help you to realise how a simple garden can be made wonderful and can give so much happiness.

Our backyard was empty and colourless. After two generations of market gardens the top soil had been washed away because the gardens were not made on level areas. Because heavy clay made it impossible to dig I decided it would be a good idea to make a garden on top of the clay. I had a 20 cm concrete wall made around the proposed garden area and imported weed-free soil, which proved to be useless because without lots of fertiliser nothing grew successfully.

It was then that the inspiration came to cover that sick soil with lucerne hay and compost. What strange instructions, but I took notice and ordered a bale of lucerne hay (when it was delivered the carrier asked: 'Where do you keep your horse?'). I covered the area with pads of lucerne hay, a sprinkling of blood and bone, a 20 cm layer of teased straw, plus a further sprinkle of blood and bone (you can also use chicken manure), and finally about 10 cm of compost. The No Dig garden was now ready for planting zucchini, silver beet, carrot seeds and tomato seedlings. The plants grew with amazing results and were strong and healthy.

The next inspiration was to make a No Dig garden on top of an area of grass.

Make sure you have everything you need before you begin, as this makes it possible to have an 'instant garden'.

❖ Make a frame of whatever material is available—be it timber, old sleepers, or concrete bricks—around an area to give an easily workable, good sized garden.

❖ Cover the grass inside the frame with a layer of newspaper 5 mm or more deep, overlapping well—do not use coloured paper or cardboard.

❖ Cover the newspaper with pads of lucerne hay as they come off the bale.

❖ Water the hay layer lightly (each layer should be lightly watered).

❖ Sprinkle the hay with blood and

bone fertiliser or chicken manure.

❖ Cover the area with about 20 cm of teased loose straw.

❖ Sprinkle this layer with blood and bone fertiliser or chicken manure.

❖ Tip a circle of good compost about 10 cm deep and about 45 cm across where seeds or seedlings are to be planted. (If enough compost is available then cover the whole area.)

❖ Plant seeds or seedlings then water gently.

Hey presto, you have created your first No Dig garden!

The green tops of the potatoes push up through the straw.

Lift the straw to check on the potatoes.

Store the potatoes unwashed.

A bumper crop!

Continue to keep your garden moist; in hot weather it helps to cover the seeds with paper or light hessian during the day, taking it off at night. Cover seedlings with an upside-down flower pot during the day.

A No Dig potato garden is exciting. Go to your greengrocer and select ten good round potatoes with 'eyes'. Place one potato in the centre of each pad of lucerne hay and cover with four handfuls of compost followed by a layer of about 20 cm of teased loose straw. Water gently and well.

After a few weeks the potatoes will push up through the straw. As they grow make sure that they are covered adequately with straw or grass cuttings, otherwise 'greening' might take place, making them inedible. When the tops have died down, remove the top layer of straw and your potatoes will be ready for harvesting. Store in a dry place (do not wash them) until you are ready to enjoy your lovely home-grown potatoes.

Because this garden is above ground level there is good drainage in wet weather. After harvesting replace the top

The first garden in a bedstead.

straw and cover it with compost. The soil is ready for you to plant beans, lettuce or any above ground vegetable, such as sweet corn, broad beans or tomatoes.

COMPOST SOIL

If good compost is provided, plants grow quicker, are much more flavoursome, and are better for us. Working with good healthy soil makes gardening a pleasant hobby or interest. The worms that are so precious in the garden have plenty of work to do converting the humus to rich living soil. Take a handful of soil and see the tiny white thread-like baby worms: put one under a magnifying glass or microscope and see the particles of brown already in its body.

If a permanent compost bin is required, this design is a long lasting bin—easy to use.

All creatures we find in the garden make gardening interesting and it is fun to learn their habits.

WATERING

Watering a garden is a very special task. (Over the years I have made quite a study of watering my garden.) It varies according to the different seasons and the plants that grow during those seasons, so take notice of the plants' habits and the amount of water they require.

After a very hot summer's day I have the greatest pleasure in going to the garden when the soil is cool (at about 10 p.m.), turning the tap to about half pressure, and adjusting the hose nozzle to allow the water to fall down on the garden like rain. The resulting cool fresh aroma of the garden is a delight. If going to the garden at night be sure to cover your legs and wear your garden shoes—sometimes the creepy crawlies wander about.

IDEAS FOR THE GARDEN

I received an inquiry from a woman in Brisbane asking if the No Dig garden could be made for people with disabilities. Until this inquiry I had not thought seriously about it. Jeanette, one of my helpers, mentioned the inquiry to her uncle, who suggested making a garden on an old bedstead. My neighbour had an old bedstead on which he dried his home-grown onions. Some ninety years earlier it had been a hospital bed, and after much persuasion I was allowed to use it. Little did I know it was to become so famous.

A row of old palings was placed on the wire of the bedstead to form a base and sides. It was covered with layers of newspaper, lucerne hay, blood and bone, straw, more fertiliser and was finally topped with fertiliser. The vegetable seeds that were planted on the bedstead grew into beautiful healthy plants. This method of gardening without digging or the need to bend over has wonderful possibilities for people with certain disabilities or for elderly people, as it allows them to share the healing benefits of contact with nature.

OCCUPATIONAL THERAPY

A group of Occupational Therapists from the Julie Farr Geriatric Centre in Adelaide wanted to give many of their charges a

Raised gardens at the Julie Farr Centre, Adelaide.

new programme of thought and I was invited to demonstrate how a garden without digging was made.

The first No Dig garden at this centre was made for the television cameras on an old hospital traymobile placed on the lawn of the Centre.

It was wonderful to see the happy faces of the twelve people involved when they were given newspaper, lucerne hay, straw, fertiliser and compost to handle. They were responsible for making the garden themselves, and planted small seedlings alongside new seeds.

Dr Farmer, the principal of the Centre, observed the reaction and was most impressed by the active participation and obvious pleasure the residents found in handling the various elements involved in making the garden. He commented that he could 'see the wonderful therapy of this garden'.

Two years later, when I visited the Julie Farr Centre, I was overwhelmed to see the beautiful No Dig gardens that had been made by some of the residents in the sunshine of the open recreation area on the first level of the seven-storey building. The head gardener had made panels of concrete covered with pebblecrete about 90 cm high to be used for the walls.

This was a tremendous experience, all because a young therapist could visualise the pleasure derived from mother nature.

Mrs Dawn Bennett from the Spastic Centre in Brisbane worked with many people with disabilities, and she thought it might be a good idea to have some No Dig gardens. While many people could only watch the flowers grow, others were able to be actively involved in the growth and selling of seedlings and some vegetables. Their first garden was made on an old table with sides built up about 20 cm, with holes drilled in the tabletop to allow drainage. Other gardens were made in various containers, and they were all a success. One girl had a special garden of her own, at wheelchair height, in which she grew only strawberries, which she loved to eat.

A delegation from China visited the centre and were particularly interested in the therapeutic effects of such gardens.

Before you start your garden, sit quietly in a bright spot. With pen and paper plan your garden according to the space and position you have available, remembering that vegetables and flowers enjoy sunshine. Also, remember there are many ideas for the type of garden you can make in the section **More Ideas for the Garden** (p. 48).

When planning your garden, take into account the location of water supply, compost bin, tools and, most importantly, who will help you. To be able to share your garden with a kindly, kindred spirit adds much to the enjoyment of a garden. If you have no family to help, why not find someone nearby who would enjoy the pleasures with you?

Now I am going to take you for a walk in a garden. It's early in the morning. Just relax, close your eyes and let your mind wander about the garden.

A POEM SENT TO ME BY SOMEONE WHO HAD PLEASURE VISITING MY GARDEN.

THE CORN AND THE LILIES

Said the corn to the lilies
Press not my feet,
You are only idlers
Neither corn nor wheat
Can one earn a living just by being
  sweet?

Naught answered the lilies
Neither yes, nor nay
Only they grow sweeter
All the live-long day
Till at last the Master chanced to
  pass that way.

Whilst his tired disciples
Rested at his feet
And the proud corn rustled
Bidding them to eat
Children, said the Master, the life is
  more than meat.

Consider the lilies
How beautiful they grow
Never king had such glory
And yet no toil they know
Oh happy were the lilies because he
  loved them so.

Unknown

IS THERE ANYTHING AS LOVELY

Is there anything as lovely as a garden
    in the morning?
As a garden in the morning when the sun
    begins to rise?
When his face peeps out all rosy from
    beneath a misty blanket
And he stretches golden fingers out and
    pokes them in my eyes

Is there anything as peaceful as a
    garden in the morning,
When the wind is still asleep and
    only breathes a gentle sigh?
And a mother bird is chirping to a timid
    little fledgling
As, with mother-love unlimited, she
    teaches him to fly

Is there anything as peaceful as a
    garden in the morning,
When leaf patterns smudge a shadow
    on a sun-warmed crazy path,
And a little spartan sparrow, heedless
    of approaching footsteps,
Throws bright diamonds all around him
    as he takes his morning bath?

Is there anything as lovely as a garden
    in the morning
When the flowers have a freshness and
    the grass is wet with dew,
And everything is quiet and the world
    seems to be waiting
For the sun to lift his eternal flame and
    climb his dome of blue?

No . . . there's nothing quite so lovely as
    a garden in the morning,
When spider webs are draped like fairy
    curtains on the trees,
The quietness is like a prayer in scented
    incense rising,
And like a benediction is the humming of
    the bees.

Oh! I walk so very softly in my garden
    in the morning,
And I thank God for these moments ere
    the household is astir
And I bend to touch a flower or smell a
    lilac's perfume,
I feel in this dear solitude . . . that God is
    walking there.

Unknown

THE GIFT OF LOVE

John Ryan is multi-physically handicapped, and is blessed with a fine intelligence, a delightful sense of fun and the most wonderful gift of all, the gift of love. His compassion for suffering humanity and his understanding of human frailty transcends his own disabilities. John has produced a book of beautiful thoughts in verse, some of which follow. Proceeds from the sale of this book are donated to the United Nations Children's Fund.

THE OLD TREE

See that old tree
It has many uses.
Children play in it;
They make friends in that tree.
When they fall in love
They go back to that tree.
When they have children
They will go back to that tree.

BY THE RIVER

I like to sit by the river,
Where there are old trees standing watch;
Where the green grass is a mat by the river;
And birds sing their songs of joy;
When I sit by the river
I think
How little we men are.

I WALK BY THE SEA

When I walk by the sea
I think of what I would do -
If only I could have this or that.
Then the sea comes over my feet,
How lovely it is.
It is the little things that mean
so much to us.

VEGETABLE GARDENS

In a No Dig garden there will always be something growing if the best plant, vegetable, or flower is allowed to go to seed.

Happiness grows from a very small seed
So plant a few each day —
They germinate with amazing speed
And flower in a beautiful way

A salad or cooked vegetable is possible every day of the year—experiment, have fun, enjoy your garden. The following have been grown at some time in my No Dig garden: celery, lettuce, leeks, chinese spinach, mustard lettuce, silver beet, chives, tomatoes, cucumbers, carrots, parsnips, zucchini, choko, beans, rhubarb, peas, potatoes, sweet potatoes, artichokes, broad beans, all types of herbs, strawberries, and other vegetables I fancied.

The No Dig garden is ideal for growing vegetables, but there are several other important points to consider before embarking on your vegetable patch:

Light requirements

Vegetables respond well to light, and for this reason you must site your bed in an open sunny position. As you are aiming to provide your plants with as much direct sunlight as possible (especially in winter), it is recommended that you locate the bed as far away as possible from large trees with wide canopies and competing root systems.

Also, in summer plant corn in patches in which climbing beans can be grown using the corn as support, otherwise three stakes and wire mesh make easy support for beans and peas.

Grow a Dahlia here and there—they give shelter to the small vegetables and add colour.

Temperature requirements

Some vegetables require warmth to germinate and are very susceptible to cold weather, especially frosts. Others are cold season vegetables which grow best at low temperatures and mature during winter. It is important to know which vegetable belongs to which category and not to plant out of season. The chart on the next page will help you.

SEEDS

Remember seeds are our future food—we must cherish any seeds from old varieties which have never failed us and have gone on and on for generations. If you have any old-time varieties to grow, allow your best plant to go to seed. When dry, take off the largest heads and place them on paper until thoroughly dry before storing in a jar.

In a No Dig garden there will always be something growing if the best plant, vegetable, or flower is allowed to go to seed.

The life force in seeds varies, eg corn and wheat keep for many years whereas parsnips must be fresh; carrots are fertile for about two months, beetroot for several months. Tomato seeds vary but use these from each season.

Select your best pods of beans and peas when on the vine and tie a coloured thread of wool around selected pod and allow to dry on the plant.

Good soil with plenty of humus contains all the elements for healthy plants which in turn receive the benefit. Lightning, rain, snow and wind are all very important for healthy soil.

Hybrid seeds are lacking in the important life force which only comes into our plants from the true soil. Hybrid plants do not yield seeds that can be re-sown.

Use the following list of vegetables as a guide to beginning your vegetable garden. It includes those vegetables which are easy to grow in the home garden, and those which are popular in cooking.

Beans

Beans are a highly productive crop for the home garden. They can be grown all year round in warm regions. Dwarf beans take 8 to 10 weeks to mature and climbers about 10 to 12 weeks. There are many

TEMPERATURE REQUIREMENTS — VEGETABLES

COOL SEASON	INTERMEDIATE CLIMATE	WARM SEASON
Broad beans	Beetroot	Beans
Broccoli	Cabbage	Capsicum
Brussels sprouts	Carrot	Choko
Cauliflower	Celery	Eggplant
Onions	Leek	Potato
Peas	Lettuce	Sweet corn
Spinach	Parsnip	Sweet potato
Turnips	Radish	Tomato
	Silver beet	Vine crops

The No Dig garden is ideal for growing vegetables, as you can see from these results.

ways to cope with climbing beans—use what is available. Varieties to look out for are 'Royal Windsor' (dwarf string beans), 'Snapbean' (dwarf stringless), 'Epicure' (climber) and 'Scarlet Runner' (climbing runner beans) for cold climates.

Beetroot

Beetroot is adaptable to all climatic regions but may run to seed if sown out of season. In cooler climates sow from September to February; in temperate areas from July to March; and in the tropics most months of the year are suitable for sowing, except for the wet season. Beetroot is at its best when grown quickly, and takes only 8–10 weeks to mature. It responds well to doses of liquid fertiliser. Some popular varieties are 'Derwent Globe', 'Early Wonder' and 'Golden Apollo'.

Broad Beans

Broad beans are a cold season vegetable. They are suited to mild, temperate and cool climates and are sown from March to May and harvested in late winter and early spring. It is a tall, leafy crop and needs adequate growing space. Extra water is

Vines such as pumpkins, melons and marrow should have plenty of space. This No Dig garden was made in a hollow on rock—and pumpkins galore was the result.

not needed until seedlings emerge in about 2 weeks. Some form of support should be provided. Broad beans are useful for soil improvement. Varieties to look for are 'Roma' and 'Coles Dwarf'.

Cabbage

Cabbage is adaptable, and provides year-round cropping in all regions except tropical, where they are difficult to grow in the wet season. They require plenty of water combined with free drainage, and can be given regular

Let some carrots go to seed, to keep you in carrots next season.

side dressings of a water soluble fertiliser which has a high nitrogen content. Harvesting can begin from 8–16 weeks after sowing. Some popular varieties are 'Green Coronet' and 'Sugarloaf'.

Carrots

Carrot seeds will germinate in a wide range of temperatures. Plant from August to March and you can successively harvest them over most of the year. They should be planted in a space last used by an unrelated leaf crop. They appreciate regular deep watering.

Cauliflower

Cauliflower is a valuable winter vegetable. It needs a cool to cold climate to perform successfully, but may also be grown in mild temperate climates in coastal regions. It needs the chilling factor for the flower heads to form. It is advisable to sow the seeds in punnets in autumn and then transplant into your bed when they are about 10 cm high. As for all leafy vegetables cauliflowers require a high degree of nutrients to grow to potential. Harvest the flower heads when they are tight and solid for best quality. 'Phenomenal Early' and 'Deepheart' are two well-known varieties. Plant according to family needs.

Lettuce

Lettuce is a popular home-grown salad vegetable, and is suitable for either pot culture or to grow in your No Dig garden. They are quick growers and successive crops can be grown and harvested throughout the year. The crucial requirements for lettuce is that they are regularly and thoroughly watered and fertilised. 'Mignonette', 'Buttercrunch', 'Cos', 'Great Lakes' and 'Imperial Triumph' are popular varieties.

Peas

Peas are suitable to all climates and are easy to cultivate. Timing your sowing is important as frost may damage flowers and young pods. It is best to sow in the warm northern areas from March to July, in temperate zones from February to August, and in cold districts from June to September. Erect supports for climbing peas, but dwarf peas are happy to climb around surrounding plants and vegetables. Dwarf varieties include 'Earlicrop' and 'Melbourne Market', and a worthwhile climber to try is 'Telephone'. 'Snow Pea' and 'Sugarsnap' (edible podded varieties) are both deservedly popular.

Pumpkin

If you have ample space, pumpkins are a good vine crop to have rambling through the vegetable patch. They appreciate regular watering and fertilising during their growth period. 'Butternut' is a delicious variety to grow in the home garden.

Rhubarb

Rhubarb may be grown either from seed or from divided plants from late winter to early spring. It is better to grow rhubarb undisturbed for about 3 years, rather than replace it annually. Although it prefers full sun, semi-shade is tolerated. It requires good drainage, regular watering and generous feeding and is adaptable to all climates. To harvest, pick stalks from the outside first.

Silver beet

Silver beet is not a true spinach, but it is often called so in New South Wales and Queensland. It is a rapid grower, being mature in 10 weeks. Because of its strong and prolific leaf growth it requires large doses of fertiliser, and is deservedly popular because of its 'cut-and-come-again' quality.

This crop of silver beet at the Spastic Centre in Brisbane is not only healthy, it is also easily accessible.

Tomatoes

Tomatoes would certainly be the most popular of home-grown vegetables (even if it is, strictly speaking, a fruit). It is a warm season plant, so take care if you live in an area subject to frost. To minimise disease problems, do not plant your tomatoes where they have been planted in the previous few years. Tomatoes are best harvested when really ripe as this provides the fullest flavour. There are endless varieties of tomatoes, which are too numerous to name. The best thing to do is to browse through the nursery displays, taking note of the type you want, the condition of your garden, the climate in your area and whether you wish to grow the plant in a bed or a pot. Some popular varieties are 'Grosse Lisse' and 'Apollo'. 'Roma' is good for bottling, and 'Tiny Tim' is excellent for pot culture.

Zucchini

Zucchinis are a vine crop of the marrow family and are a warm season vegetable. They are a good plant for the home-style vegetable patch as they form low, bushy plants which take up very little space. The marrows are at their peak when they reach about 15 cm in length, so delay harvesting until then. 'President' and 'Greyzini' are two hybrids worthy of note.

Children

It is, no doubt, a good idea for children to plant vegetables which they like to eat. Some that are easily grown and appeal to children's tastes are tomatoes, lettuce, carrots, pumpkin, capsicum, snow peas and potatoes. A fruit which is easy to grow and which will delight children is the strawberry. It can be grown in the ground or in a strawberry pot, and the children can observe the way it flowers and how the flower in turn develops into a ripe, red, strawberry. They feel a real sense of achievement when—after watching their plants grow and develop, after watching little green berries form—they check the bush and there is a luscious strawberry ready to pick and eat.

Flowers

There is a need to add flowers to the vegetable garden. Having done so in my garden one young couple found such peace there they decided to have their baby christened in the garden under the lovely carob tree—a little backyard garden can be a wonderful place. A little patch of Sweet Peas for springtime colour and fragrance, a few Iceland Poppies for brilliance and the lovely open centres provide lots of pollen for the bees; Pansies give edges a charming touch while Heartsease are happy with everything that grows and give their own medicinal vibes. For summer be sure to have lovely Dahlias, especially a single one here and there—they are a great favourite with the bees and also give moving shade for small plants. The old fashioned Marigold helps protect with its strong smell and adds a lovely touch of gold flowering for a long time. I do not advocate Violets for a vegetable garden or any of the Mint family, which spread quickly and spoil the garden. All mints are best grown in pots.

TOMATOES STUFFED WITH FRESH CORN

4 ripe tomatoes
2 cobs corn, cooked
1 tablespoon chopped onion
½ green capsicum, chopped

½ teaspoon vegetable salt
approx. ¼ cup French dressing
lettuce
mayonnaise

Peel the tomatoes and remove the core. Scoop out the pulp and leave a wall a little less than 12 mm thick. Drain excess liquid out of the tomato cups. Remove corn from the cobs, add chopped tomato pulp, onion, capsicum and salt. Combine this mixture with the French dressing and use it to fill the tomato cups. Chill well and serve on lettuce and mayonnaise.

SENSES IN THE GARDEN

Sound, texture and fragrance can be highlighted in a garden, as can colour, form and design. Each season brings forth wonderfully perfumed trees, shrubs and climbers. (It is hard to imagine spring without Freesias, Stocks, or Boronia, summer without Frangipani and Mock Orange, autumn without Carnations, or winter without Violets.) Add plants with aromatic leaves to the beautifully scented flowers, and your garden will be well on the way to being a perfumed paradise. Aromatic foliage is often ignored, and many spicy, woody and lemony scents are overlooked. More attention should be paid to these plants, and the following selection will guide you to selecting plants for year-round pleasure—to grace your No Dig garden, or to plant in pots.

TEXTURE IN THE GARDEN

Every good gardener knows the value of utilising foliage texture to create interest and variation in their planting schemes. Choosing plants with foliage which either contrasts with its neighbours, or, at the other extreme, harmonises with surrounding plants is as important, if not more important, than choosing for flower colour. Harmonising plant texture by planting in groups rather than 'one of this, one of that' makes a dramatic impact.

To run your hands over a soft mound of creeping Thyme, or to gently feel the feathery foliage of German Chamomile are delights not to be missed by anyone. Both hands and feet can be recipient to garden textures. It is lovely to walk across dew-laden grass early in the morning, or to run your hands along the shrubbery, feeling all sorts of contrasting leaves and plant shapes. By feeling your plants this way you will come to know your garden intimately.

Nasturtiums
Nasturtium leaves fascinate children as they are lovely to touch, and hold droplets of water after rain showers or hosing. Nectar can be sucked from their colourful orange, yellow or red flowers, and all parts of the plant are edible.

Plants with Fragrant Flowers

Brown Boronia

An evergreen Australian native shrub, Brown Boronia forms a sparse bush to 1 m in height. The scent the brown bell-shaped flowers produce in late winter and spring is extremely beautiful, and is carried on gentle breezes.

Burkwood Virburnum

An evergreen shrub which grows 1–2 m, Burkwood Viburnum carries heads of white, delightfully fragrant flowers in spring. Cool climates are preferred.

Carnation

The latin name for carnation adequately describes the scent of this delightful perennial—*Dianthus caryophyllus*—as 'perfume resembling cloves'. The main flower display occurs in spring and autumn, but they do flower throughout the year. Carnations prefer an open, sunny position and do not like being covered by other plants.

Citrus: *lemon, orange, mandarin, lime, kumquat*

Citrus trees are a valuable addition to your garden, providing an attractive small tree, wonderfully perfumed citrus blossom and edible fruits. They are not suitable for cool highland areas where frosts may damage trees and fruit. Maximum sunlight is needed to ripen the fruit.

Daphne

A small, rounded evergreen shrub to 1 m in height, this charming plant has thick, glossy foliage and highly perfumed waxy flowers in pink or white. Daphne flowers in winter and early spring and is suitable for cool and temperate climates. If you provide it with a semi-shaded position with morning sun, good drainage and mulch over its roots to keep it cool and moist it should reward you abundantly with fragrant blossom, although it can be a temperamental plant and die suddenly.

Freesia

Freesias herald the coming of spring. They are easy to grow and are showy, with their colourful and strongly perfumed tubular flower. In nature, only the white and yellow species occur, but there are many bright colours in the modern hybrid. They flower abundantly from late winter to spring. They pick well, and add a delightful fragrance to indoor flower arrangements or posies.

Gardenia

Gardenias are handsome evergreen shrubs with sweetly scented blossoms. The perfume hangs heavily on sultry summer days. The creamy white flowers appear from November to March and the glossy deep-green leaves are a perfect foil for them.

Jonquil

Jonquils are an early spring-flowering bulb, with fragrant blooms like miniature Daffodils. They look most effective massed or in clumps, and can be left undisturbed for years to grow in the one place.

Lavender

Lavender is a shrubby perennial growing from 30–90 cm, and is evergreen with aromatic leaves. Lavender—of which there are a number of types—is native to the Mediterranean area, and dislikes being waterlogged, so provide it with free drainage and adequate water in summer. It enjoys full sun, but is fairly hardy and will withstand light frosts. Pinch back the shoots to encourage bushy growth. All Lavender flowers have a distinctive woody, aromatic scent when dried, and are used in pot-pourri and scented sachets.

Stocks

Lemon-scented Jasmine

Lemon-scented Jasmine is a warmly fragrant, twining evergreen climber which flowers in summer and autumn.

Madagascar Jasmine — *Stephanotis*

Madagascar Jasmine is a handsome creeper with glossy deep-green foliage which needs light support and training. Fragrant, white trumpet-like flowers are produced in late summer. It needs a warm, sheltered position in a temperate climaate.

Mexican Orange Blossom — *Choisa*

A small, bushy, evergreen shrub 2 m x 2 m, Mexican Orange Blossom forms a nicely rounded plant. Its leaves are pungent when bruised, and it develops a cluster of small, sweetly fragrant white flowers from early September to November. It appreciates a warm position in the garden and can be grown in all temperate regions in Australia, and in sheltered sites in areas of high elevation. It is a useful hedging plant and can be clipped into a neat shape.

Orange Jessamine — *Murraya*

An evergreen small to medium shrub with a very strong scent, Orange Jessamine carries deep glossy green leaves and perfumed flowers reminiscent of citrus blossom. The flowering period is long and during summer.

Mock Orange

Mock Orange is a delightful group of shrubs. They are deservedly popular for their lovely late spring and early summer flowers. The flowers are white, and perfumed like citrus blossom. Pruning is done after flowering and old wood should be cut back at the base.

Pinks

The foliage on this short, tufted annual is an attractive grey-green colour. It grows to 35 cm, and flowers are borne singly or in clusters, in pinks, reds, lavenders and whites. The perfume is more delicate than that of its relative, the Carnation, but even so it is well worth adding to the garden. Although Pinks may flower throughout the year, their main flush is from July to October.

Port Wine Magnolia

An evergreen rounded shrub, Port Wine Magnolia has small oval leaves, shiny green above and paler and dull beneath. The brownish flowers, hidden in the bush, appear from early September to late

November. They are sweetly and strongly perfumed, and it is a useful plant for providing background structure in your shrubbery or garden bed.

Pot Jasmine

Pot Jasmine is an exquisitely fragrant evergreen climber, lovely wafting about and best suited to open spaces. It is quite vigorous and can be used to cover fences or pergolas. It is stunning at peak flowering, when the blooms almost completely cover the foliage.

Primrose

The flowers of the primrose are a pale yellow colour with a scent similar to violets. It is lovely in wooded areas, under aged trees, or nestled into shaded positions on banks.

Star Jasmine

A moderately vigorous climber with small glossy deep green leaves, Star Jasmine carries star-like, white perfumed flowers from late October to late December.

Stocks

Stocks are a pretty annual, originating in southern Europe. Flowers have a sweet delicate fragrance, and it is a vigorous plant, growing to 50 cm tall with a brilliant colour range. Stocks won the flower of the year award in 1976.

Sweet Osmanthus

The perfume of Sweet Osmanthus has been variously described as 'a blend of Jasmine, Gardenia and ripe apricots', and as 'ripe peach'. It is a sparse shrub with glossy toothed leaves, resembling holly, and clusters of minute white flowers. The perfume is very strong, and a couple of flower sprays are adequate to perfume the whole house.

Sweet Pea

Sweet Pea is an outstandingly beautiful annual, loved for its delicate sweet perfume and for its wide range of soft and sometimes bright colours. The large pea flowers come in white, cream, pink, lavender, purple, red, maroon and scarlet, all of which are charming.

Violets

There is nothing nicer in winter than picking a tightly packed posy of sweet-smelling Violets to bring indoors and scent a room. The fragrant flowers are mostly purple but sometimes white, and are borne above the foliage in late winter and spring. They are not too fussy about conditions, but regular watering and good drainage are advisable. They prefer a position in semi-shade.

Wallflower

Wallflowers are annuals with a wonderful exotic fragrance reminiscent of spices of the Orient. The flowers come in a large range of beautiful colours, from yellow, orange and white, to red, brown and crimson. The long, narrow leaves arch gracefully and the plant is bushy: dwarf to tall types are available. They flower late winter and early spring. Wallflowers are

effective when massed in beds or in rockeries. They are a good cut flower for indoor decoration.

Wax Flower — *Hoya*

Wax Flower is an evergreen twining climber with thick shiny mid-green leaves; a variegated form with a cream margin is also available. The clusters of pink, star-shaped flowers hang down, almost dripping with sweetly perfumed nectar in summer. The small flowers in compact clusters appear to be almost unreal and made of wax. New buds arise

Plant sweet peas and appreciate their colour, texture, and sweet perfume.

from the old flower spurs, so do not prune this climber or you will lose the flowers in the next season. It prefers a warm, sheltered position and takes well to pot culture.

PLANTS WITH AROMATIC FOLIAGE

Bottlebrush—*Callistemon citrinus*

As its name suggests, this species of Bottlebrush has foliage which, when crushed, has the scent of lemons. It forms a shrub to 3 m, on a short single trunk with many low branches forming a rounded shape. It bears a crimson bottlebrush from October through to November.

Diosma

Diosma is a low shrub to 2 m in height and spreading as wide. It has fine, soft feathery foliage with tiny flowers in purple, pink and white shades in spring. The foliage is mildly aromatic.

Eucalyptus citriodora

This species of eucalypt has a strong lemon-scent when bruised or disturbed by light winds. It is a tall, graceful tree reaching 20–30 m in ornamental plantings. Its smooth creamy-grey bark is an added attraction.

Eucalyptus nicholii

A tall, straight tree to 15 m with a conical crown of slender branches with blueish-green narrow leaves. As its common name, 'Willow-Leafed Peppermint', suggests, the foliage has a peppermint aroma when crushed.

Most other Eucalypts have leaves which are aromatic when bruised due to the presence of oil glands in the foliage.

Lemon-scented Tea-tree

A small native tree to 5 m with a short single trunk with rough papery bark. The narrow light green leaves have a strong but

The native grevillea is beloved by birds, and adds a splash of green to any garden.

pleasant lemon scent when crushed. The tree also produces masses of small white flowers in December and January. This is a small tree well worth having in a garden and while it has a tendency to be sparse, regular pruning improves density.

Purple Mint Bush

Another Australian native with a wonderful aroma from the leaf, this time the scent of mint. It is an evergreen shrub to 3 m with delightful small, soft foliage and violet or purple flowers in spring. Other species are also available.

Pelargonium

Pelargoniums are very useful plants and can be used as groundcover, edging plants, or in pots and hanging baskets. They provide not only a wonderful range of scents but also many useful flavours for cooking. Species vary in size and although the flowers are small and undistinguished they appear in copious numbers.

Take a walk in the bush and enjoy the wonders of creation.

SOUND IN THE GARDEN

Plants can be grown to attract birds into the garden. Banksias, Acacias and Grevilleas are good varieties for attracting nectar-eating birds like honeyeaters. Many parrots are attracted by plants with seeds.

The garden can also be a place of different sounds, not only the sweet song of the birds, but plants can rustle in the wind, and windchimes made of timber, metal, bamboo, or shells create varied sounds. The sight or sound of a waterfall in a garden brings forth an image of peacefulness and tranquillity. A bird bath is a must, as is a hanging food tray. Such additions to your garden are items of particular interest to children.

Birds and insects

It is not only the sound of birds which enhance the garden but insects as well. Bees, frogs, cicadas and crickets all produce memorable sounds. A swarm of bees feeding on the nectar-producing shrubs create a wonderful low 'hum' in the garden and they produce honey and play an important role in pollination and cross-fertilisation of plants at the same time; and who could forget the deafening drone of cicadas on summer evenings?

Although all these animals contribute, it is the various trills, screeches, chirps, or laughs of birds that are the most appreciated garden sounds. To attract

Birds need water and shelter in the garden to make it a safe, comfortable place for them.

birds to your garden, you should plant nectar-producing trees and shrubs such as Grevilleas, Banksias, Eucalypts, Correas, Boronias, Callistemons and some of the Acacias. These provide the birds with a basic food source, but birds also need insects and other garden creatures, such as grasshoppers, worms, cicadas and spiders.

It is the various trills, screeches, chirps and laughs of birds that are the most appreciated garden sounds...

No poisonous sprays should be used in any garden which will be visited by many birds. Some find food (insects) amongst the low-growing plants whilst others hang upside down to sip nectar from the brightly coloured flowers. Lizards sun themselves and sometimes beautifully patterned butterflies add their splendour to the garden.

Birds also need water and shelter in the garden for it to become a safe, comfortable environment for them. If you don't have a natural watercourse (creek or gully) through your garden, a bird bath or shallow water trough in a safe place away from predators such as cats is sufficient.

Finally, create dense thickets of shrubs and tangled creepers for safe nesting in a secluded part of the garden. Plant the larger Grevilleas, Melaleucas, Prostantheras, Bottlebrushes and Banksias. This natural and bushy portion of your garden will become a refuge for birds. They can nest there, and materials for nest making such as bark, pieces of vine, grasses and dead leaves are readily available on site.

NOISE-MAKING PLANTS

Sound is a sensual pleasure we tend to overlook when selecting plants and trees.

It is an added dimension to the garden which should not be neglected.

One tree readily available to Australian gardeners which creates a wonderful rustling or clattering sound in strong wind is the native Eucalypt. Its leaves have a dry, leathery quality, so that when the wind rubs them together a papery-sounding rustling occurs.

One of the most beautiful sounding trees is the River She-oak (*Casuarina cunninghamiana*), and gentle breezes through the foliage create a whispering or gentle sighing.

Bamboo is another effective plant for making noise in the garden, producing a rustling in light wind. If planting this in the garden concerns you because it spreads so easily, try growing it in a pot. A large, wide, bowl-shaped container suits bamboo well.

The European Aspen is a lovely rustling tree. Its small roundish leaves, broader than wide, with large rounded teeth are held by slender flattened stalks. It is this which permits the constant movement of the leaves and hence the sound.

If you live in a hot tropical or warm temperate climate, plant a grove of palms and you will be rewarded with their distinctive rustling sound when the fronds clatter on breezy days.

CREATING SOUND IN THE GARDEN

There are several ways to add sounds to your garden apart from using natural sounds. Water features are invaluable in garden making, because of the movement, light and reflective properties of water and also because of the gentle sound it makes when moving. In addition, it cools the garden in hot conditions. If you have a natural source of water in your garden you are very lucky indeed, but for those of us who don't, informal or formal pools can be created. Movement and sound can be added by including a fountain which sprays gently from within the pond, or by creating a cascade from one level to another in a series of ponds.

Safety should always be a primary consideration in designing water features in the garden, so:

❖ eliminate informal pools with no defined edge in the garden proper

❖ choose formal ponds or pools with raised sides or edges, and

❖ make the pond of minimum depth (60 cm is sufficient for an ornamental pool).

If pump-driven waterfall and fountains are desired a pump would need to be installed and expert advice should be sought for its design and installation.

Wind chimes

Wind chimes and bells make delightful sounds in the garden. Many different types of materials are used for chimes, from tubular steel to pottery. Each makes a different sound, so it is necessary to listen to a variety before you choose one you like.

Sound adds another dimension to the garden—why not add some wind chimes!

COLOUR IN THE GARDEN

Busy Lizzie

Busy Lizzie are easily grown plants which last for a long time and self seed, thereby producing more plants for the children. The flowers come in many bright colours.

Cosmos

The daisy-like flowers of Cosmos will be an attractive feature in a child's garden. The plant grows quite tall, and is easily cultivated by just casting the seed onto the soil.

English Daisy

The small 'pom-pom' flower heads of English Daisy will delight children. Colours include white, pink and now red in the new 'Gemstone Collection'.

Granny's Bonnets

The unusual flower of Granny's Bonnets resembles old-fashioned bonnets, and will provide interest for many as it is a prolific self-seeding annual which will provide plants for years.

Enhance a corner by cramming it with colour.

Pansies

Pansies are popular plants with children, probably because markings on the flowers remind them of little faces. They are easy to grow and have a gorgeous colour range.

Petunias

Petunias are reliable and colourful plants which put on a good show without requiring too much care. Varieties are available in an extremely wide colour range including stripes, and some have frilly petals.

Polyanthus

Polyanthus are bright, cheery plants with a dense cluster of flowers. They come in a wide variety of colours, some in one colour and some with a star of contrasting colour in the centre. If you are lucky enough to find *Polyanthus 'vulgaris'*, the true Primrose, it has a delightful perfume.

Poppies

Who could resist these bright little beacons in the depth of winter? The solitary flowers are borne on long stalks and come

An iris in all its beauty.

in red, violet, yellow, tangerine, pink and white. They last well when cut.

Snapdragons

People love squeezing Snapdragon flowers and watching them 'pop'. They are colourful, densely foliaged plants, and tall, medium and dwarf varieties are available. They have a faint perfume.

Stocks

The scent of Stocks will appeal. Dwarf, medium and tall varieties are available and there is a wide colour range.

Endymion hispanicus (Spanish Bluebell)

JOHN'S STORY

John was a student at the Deaf and Blind Children's Centre, North Rocks. They have very caring teachers to help the children staying at the centre and one of the teachers, who I have named Samson, helped John with his garden on the old bedstead.

John loves gardens, and with Samson's help he was able to create a garden on a bedstead. The plants grown in the garden were very healthy with different shaped leaves, varied textures as well as distinct smells, helping John to learn more about the variety of plants that can be grown in a garden.

Other children at the Centre have been helped with gardens by Samson, and they have been able to plant trees and shrubs in an area where nothing has grown before. The children enjoy touching the various leaves and learning the different fragrances which are an essential part of any garden.

John's garden

HERBS

Culinary herbs are used widely in gardens as they are both attractive as plant specimens and useful in food preparation and flavouring. Herbs are usually positioned together in a bed as close as possible to the kitchen to enable quick access when cooking, although there is no reason why they should not take their place in the garden at large. They can be grown in pots, used as hedges or edging plants or, indeed, as part of the general shrubbery. They can also be used as groundcover or to replace lawn. Thyme, marjoram and chamomile make delightfully fragrant walkways. If substituting an existing lawn with a thyme cover choose one of the varieties of *Thymus serpyllum* which forms a dense mat.

Herbs have many uses and need not be confined to herb beds, however, if you are

HOT, DRY, SUNNY SITE

Mediterranean herbs
(Grey, shrubby foliage)

Bay	Rue
Catmint	Rosemary
Cistus	Sage
Hyssop	Santolinas
Jerusalem Sage	Thyme
Lavender	Woodworm
Marjoram	

COOL, DAMP SITE

(Green and herbaceous)

Angelica	Lemon balm
Balm	Lovage
Basil	Meadowsweet
Bergamot	Mint
Borage	Parsley
Chives	Sweet Cicily
Cress	Tansy
Fennel	Tarragon
Feverfew	Turmeric

going to mix them in the garden it is wise to ensure the habitat is suited to each particular herb. There are basically two types of herbs—those which like a 'Mediterranean' climate (hot, dry and sunny), and those which prefer damper and shadier sites. The table will help you identify which herb belongs to which category.

The following herbs include those most commonly used and those most readily available at local nurseries. Specialist herb nurseries should be able to provide the enthusiast with a wide range of more unusual herbs.

Basil

Common Basil grows to about 50 cm high, with glossy green leaves and a spike of white flowers. Basil loves the warmer spots in the garden. Bush Basil is a good specimen for a pot as it is compact. In cooking, Basil goes extremely well with tomato, and can be used in tomato soups, sauces, salads, and to make pesto.

Borage

Borage is an annual, varying in height from 30–90 cm, with coarse, hairy leaves and stems. Borage is hardy and easily grown. It is a very beautiful plant. The little bright blue flowers attract bees in profusion. Sit nearby when they are in full bloom and enjoy listening to the hum of the bees. The flowers add a delightful touch to salads and can be sugar coated for cake decorations. Borage is known as the herb of gladness. It may self sow, so it will provide you with plants over a period of years. It can be used to flavour drinks and punches, and has a pleasant cucumber flavour.

Chamomile

Chamomile grows to 30 cm high, with delightfully feathery leaves of the purest green and white daisy-like flowers. It can be grown in sun or semi-shade. A soothing herbal tea may be made from the flowers, and it is also reputed to ease anxiety and soothes and works as a sedative for children suffering from colic or earache. Some people may be allergic to Chamomile. Finally, it can also be used as a hair rinse.

Chives

Chives are a type of onion. The leaves will grow 25–30 cm high, but may be kept trimmed to a lower height. The bright green, slender leaves are fine and hollow and taste of Garlic. Full sun is preferred but Chives do tolerate partial shade. Chives can be used in most savoury dishes.

Dill

Dill has finely cut, feathery blue-green leaves and small yellow flowers. Seeds can be sown in spring or early summer. The leaves have a pungent, bitter-sweet taste, and the seeds can also be used for flavouring. Dill prefers full sun, and the leaves and seeds are ripe for fresh use in summer.

Garlic

Garlic has flat green leaves which grow to 1 m and die back after flowering, and has purple and white flowers. The bulblets should be planted in full sun, and provided with adequate water in a well-drained position. Garlic is used in many recipes, and is also credited with having health-giving properties.

Lemon Balm

Balm grows to 1 m, and its attractive, toothed green leaves have a strong lemon scent. The plant has small white flowers. It is a good herb to grow in a pot, and has many culinary uses.

Lemon Verbena

The Lemon Verbena shrub has lemon-scented leaves and needs to be grown in a warm sheltered position in full sun. The narrow lemony leaves can be used in pot-pourri and as a herbal tea. Pinch out new shoots to encourage bushy growth, and mulch around the base in winter to give the roots shelter from the cold.

Lovage

The dark, glossy green leaves of Lovage—resembling celery leaves—make for an attractive plant. It is strongly aromatic and produces yellow flowers. It is used in savoury dishes, with salads and to make herbal teas.

Marjoram

Marjoram grows 30–40 cm high, and has oval leaves with tiny white or purplish flowers. It thrives in full sun but must not be allowed to dry out, so attention should be paid to watering it.

Mint: *Peppermint, Eau de Cologne, Apple Mint, Pennyroyal, Spearmint*

Many types of Mint are available. They spread by runners and are therefore suitable plants for pots. Each species varies in height from low groundcover to bushes which reach 1 m in height. Flower colours vary from white to pink, lilac and purple. Mint is a very useful herb for flavouring drinks, salads and peas, and for infusing in teas. They grow easily in a moist, sunny, warm position.

Nasturtium

The Nasturtium has its origins in southern and central America. It is a strong climber with long twining stems, and is available with pink, white, yellow, orange, scarlet and red flowers. All parts of the plant are edible, and can be used creatively.

Oregano

Oregano is a mat-forming perennial growing to 75 cm, and the long oval leaves are dark green and can be either smooth or hairy. Its pungent flavour complements both vegetarian and meat dishes, and is traditionally associated with Italian, Spanish and South American cooking.

Parsley

Parsley is one of the most popular of herbs, and adapts well to container planting. It has a curly deep-green leaf, and tolerates both full sun and half shade. When established, plants respond well to regular applications of a liquid plant food. When harvesting Parsley pick the leaves from the

Herbs have many uses and need not be confined to herb beds: plant them in pots and keep them near the kitchen.

outside of the plant, as new growth takes place from the centre of the crown.

Rosemary

The dense leafy branches of Rosemary give it a somewhat spiky outline. The leaves have a pine-like fragrance, and Rosemary is a very useful plant for Australia as it enjoys full sun. This is a versatile herb, and can flavour vinegars or soups, stuff meat, or enhance sauces.

Sage

Sage is a semi-woody shrub growing to 50 cm, with rough-textured, long, grey-green leaves. It has vertical spikes of flowers in blue, white, or pink. Full sun is required, and these plants will tolerate quite dry conditions. It is traditionally used in stuffings and meat dishes but, as with all herbs, this is just a start for other inventive approaches.

Thyme

Thyme is a small bushy plant related to the Mint family and grown for its distinctive, warm aroma. Thyme is a plant of the sunny slopes of the Mediterranean, and is traditionally used in bouquet garni and in meat stuffings with Sage and onion.

ZUCCHINI WITH HERBS

500 g zucchini

1 small onion, chopped

1 clove garlic

¼ cup butter

2 dessertspoons vegetable oil

1 teaspoon vegetable salt seasoning

1 teaspoon sweet basil

½ bay leaf

5 tomatoes, peeled and cut up

2 dessertspoons chopped parsley

Wash and cut zucchini into thin rounds. Do not peel. Sauté onion and garlic in the melted butter and oil until slightly brown. Add zucchini and all seasonings and herbs, together with ½ cup boiling water. Cook a few minutes. Add tomatoes. Cook a few minutes more. Add chopped parsley and serve.

Serves: 8

TEACHING CHILDREN TO LOVE
THE GARDEN

There is a wonderful variety of creatures, both good and bad, to be found in a garden. Children can learn that there is a common snail, as well as a cannibal snail that eats the common snail; that there is a magical process of the butterfly cycle, from an egg to a caterpillar to a butterfly. Give a child a magnifying glass to see just how beautiful the tiny flowers on weeds are.

Melissa is washing the carrots and *learning the delights of the garden.*

The wonders of creation are beyond one's comprehension.

The child should have the responsibility of selecting the plants, preparing the garden, planting, watering, fertilising and weeding. For children who are visually impaired, plants with fragrant flowers or aromatic foliage, or those with interesting leaf textures are the best choice. For children with restricted mobility annuals are easy to care for, and can be readily grown in small beds, or in pots, as will be discussed in the section on container planting. Other suggestions for plants and methods children will enjoy are scattered throughout the book.

When in Brisbane recently I visited a school where blind children are integrated with sighted children. Try to imagine my experience when two pretty little blind six year olds were asked: 'Would you like to read to Esther a story about the dinosaur?'

Using the brailler.

To see their dear little fingers reading braille was tremendous.

They had a dinosaur's cave made from hessian. A big cushion was on the floor and pictures of toys and dinosaurs abounded. I was invited to go into the cave, where growly noises were made to frighten me—such fun and happiness was a joy to experience.

The older class showed great interest in their lesson on the food chain. The special class was made up of two blind children, two partially blind and one sighted child, as well as the teacher.

Another delightful experience was to be invited to the home of a gentleman who lost his sight as a child of six. It was explained to me how difficult it is to learn to be blind after being sighted. Special schools and very special people are required to help the adjustment in such a situation. That gentleman has become a good pianist, and now teaches blind children to play.

When visiting New Zealand several years ago it was my pleasure to stay with a family who had a lovely

The dinosaur cave!

Reading braille music

daughter who became blind at six years of age following an illness. Her achievements are worth telling. After learning to be blind she became an excellent pupil right through her schooldays with the help of a very good friend: a guide dog was her constant companion. After leaving school she became a very efficient operator in the dark room of a local photographer. She was also secretary of the local garden club.

WHAT CAN LITTLE HANDS DO?

Children can have a lot of fun in a garden. They can plant seeds and watch plants grow from the seeds; they can see the busy bees at work, put down crumbs for the birds, wash the vegetables that have come straight from the earth, learn about the good and bad weeds or take a flower to a friend, young or old. They can learn about the various creatures we find in our garden—the beautiful butterflies, the wriggly worms. Hands and feet can touch the earth and feel the different flowers and plants: they can also learn how to water the garden to help the thirsty plants grow big and strong.

It is very important to commence teaching a child—whether they have a disability or not—to know the wonders

and beauty of creation. To feel the soft petals of a flower without hurting the flower . . . to touch the warm earth . . . to feel gentle raindrops on skin . . . to watch the trees in the wind: these are all wonderful learning experiences.

The little girl pictured below is dropping water onto a Nasturtium leaf and watching the little balls of water slithering about on the leaf.

MIRACLE OF SPRING

There was a miracle of loaves and fishes
A miracle of water turned to wine
Through the bare earth a little leaf blade
pushes
Slim as a sword and delicate and fine

From a brown seed no larger than a pinpoint
A leaf, a stem, a bud, a flower and then
From flower a seed in rhythmic rotation
To leaf and stem and bud and flower again.

There was a miracle of loaves and fishes
But I have seen the miracle of spring
The wonder that is life itself unfolding
I have no room for doubt of anything.

Unknown

Trinity discovers the possibilities for fun in the garden, and a nasturtium leaf and water is all she needs

MORE IDEAS FOR THE GARDEN

*Remember that gardens are not made by
sitting in the shade and saying Oh how
beautiful—plenty of love and care are needed.*

COMPANION PLANTING

Experiment and have fun in your garden—
a self-sown seed usually finds its own
companion.

Celery

When self sown celery decides its own
companions such as leeks and potatoes. I
have found it growing in the grass and
even in the cracks of concrete.

Leeks

Leeks are growing around most of my
garden.

Nasturtiums

Nasturtiums are excellent, having a strong
aromatic essence which passes through the
roots into soil, thus benefiting other plants.
They are also reputed to deter aphids and
other pests. The white butterfly is attracted to
nasturtiums for laying eggs, and the resulting
caterpillar is easily seen and removed.

Cabbages

The cabbage-white butterfly is attracted to
the smell of the cabbage, but if you plant
marigolds with them they will disguise the
smell of cabbage.

Lupins

Lupins are a well-known green manure
crop, which when dug in increase
nitrogen in the soil. Added to this, they
are a very pretty flowering plant. Save
the seed of the best of your Lupins for,
although they are perennials, they fade
out and it is necessary to treat them
as an annual and replace them each
year.

Heartsease

I love to see Heartsease in the garden, and
everything is happy to have their
company.

Forget-me-nots

Forget-me-nots are good companion plants
as they give mulch and provide shelter for
bacteria, which is useful to the soil. They
are very easy to thin out and can be shared
with friends. Put a couple of plants in
pots.

Sweet corn

Sweet corn makes a good companion for
climbing beans which enjoy climbing up
the stalk.

Onions

Any of the onion family are distasteful to peas, and are not good companions to them.

Herbs

Herbs are beneficial in every garden whether they are grown with flowers or with vegetables. For example Marjoram and Basil are good with tomatoes, and when crushed also repels flies; Coriander, Marigolds, Calendula and Garlic all repel aphids, as do onions and Chives; Lemon and Lime Balm attract bees; and both ants and aphids dislike Mint. Pyrethrum is used as an insect repellant, and Feverfew is not only pretty, its aromatic foliage also makes it an insect repellant.

Some herbs, too, add vigour to surrounding plants. Yarrow has this property, and Borage has deep roots which bring leached calcium and potassium up to plant level, and as its leaves decay these minerals are made available for its companion plants. Valerian makes phosphorous more available to its companions and also attracts earthworms.

This well-planned garden, with wheelchair access and raised beds, is at the Pomeroy Hospital nursing home in Perth.

WHEELCHAIR ACCESS

If the gardener moves around in a wheelchair, paths need to be smooth and wide enough for the wheelchair, with ramps to move to different levels. Raised garden beds make it easier for people who cannot bend over. As well as the bedstead approach mentioned earlier, there are other ways of building a garden.

Garden beds can be made as part of a retaining wall, breaking the starkness of the wall with splashes of colour, creating interest and endless pleasure. The garden

If the gardener moves around in a wheelchair, paths need to be smooth and wide enough for the wheelchair, with ramps to move to different levels.

is at a comfortable level to stand and work and is not very wide, making it easier to reach the back of the garden bed.

A garden shed with benches at wheelchair height is great: it can become your own den. A chair or wheelchair placed under the bench means that the work area is easily reached. Pots or timber boxes can be used for growing a variety of shade plants, including ferns. Tools can be stored on the shelves where they are always ready to use.

PLANTS IN POTS

Many different species of plant can now be grown effectively in pots. For those people who are not mobile enough to produce a No Dig garden, growing annuals, vegetables and shrubs in pots is a solution. For people with disabilities consideration must be given to the weight and moveability of the pot, and to methods of watering.

You should aim to have the containers as light and as easy to move as possible. For those who like the terracotta look, the new range of 'Terra-pots' is ideal. These are plastic but look like terracotta and are made in many different shapes from wide shallow bowls to the traditional deep pot.

A therapy garden in the Banksia Centre, Canberra.

There are many very attractive pots available, and a wide variety of plants can be grown in them.

There is also a fibreglass pot available which has the appearance of concrete but is very lightweight. Hanging baskets lined with bark or fibre provide a relatively light container in which to grow trailing plants. Although these suggestions are helpful in keeping weight down, once the potting mix has been added to your container it becomes heavier and awkward to handle. The job of moving and watering plants needs to be made easier for people with mobility problems.

To make a pot easier to move you could attach casters to the bottom of a wooden planter box and place your pot inside the planter. This makes your plant more mobile and more attractive. Otherwise, you could arrange several plants on a low trolley with wheels or casters.

The following list may help you to choose suitable specimens for gardening in pots.

Azaleas

Azaleas make perfect pot specimens because of their shallow root system. Azaleas provide a good splash of colour in the spring, even a tiny plant in a pot rewards you with masses of blooms, so really they are superb container plants.

Bulbs

Try bulbs massed on their own or group them with other plants. Crocus, Hyacinth, Ipheion, Bluebells, Grape Hyacinth and Snowdrops are all suitable for small pots. For larger containers Ranunculus, Tulips, Daffodils, Jonquils, Hippeastrum, Agapanthus and Clivea are effective. Tulips

For those people not mobile enough to produce a No Dig garden, growing plants in pots is a solution.

To make a pot easier to move, you could attach casters to the bottom.

are lovely crammed together in a wide, shallow pot with Alyssum frothing over the sides. You could perhaps combine Daffodils or Jonquils with Floss Flower.

Bulbs, too, are fascinating plants for children to learn about, the bulb itself being the entire food storage unit for the plant. Freesias are foolproof and provide a delightful spring perfume. Others which would appeal to children are Jonquils, Ipheion, Bluebells and Grape Hyacinths.

Citrus

Citrus trees in pots are wonderful for many reasons. They have attractive evergreen foliage and heavenly scented blossoms, and fruit which is both decorative and edible. The smaller growing kumquats are the most obvious choice for a tub, while mandarins are a good choice for a large tub in a sunny position.

Natives

Lillypillies are shrubby plants that take well to container growing and appreciate being pruned. Once pruned, their fresh, reddish new growth is a delight, and they also produce a lovely oval berry in late summer and autumn.

Containers and benches are used efficiently in Peter Meagher's garden (also see pp 60–61)

Pot plants can be displayed in all sorts of interesting ways.

The native Rhododendron pots up effectively and the cluster of rich bell-shaped flowers is spectacular in autumn.

The Brown Boronia is easier to grow in a pot than in the ground as you can control the water supply and its perfume is, in my opinion, the loveliest of all the scented shrubs.

The little purple Native Daisy is a pretty spillover plant for a shallow pot.

Vegetables

Most vegetables can be grown in pots providing you place them in a sunny position. An ideal tomato for containers is 'Dwarf Cherry' which has an abundance of small, decorative fruit, a bushy habit and does not require staking. Carrots can be grown in a deep pot and lettuce massed in a low, shallow trough are most attractive and can be harvested in a matter of weeks after planting seedlings. Nurseries now sell several different varieties of lettuce in one punnet which enables you to pick lettuce over a long period of time because each type develops at a different rate and provides you with a variety in taste as well. Snow peas can be planted in a long oblong trough and placed against a sunny balcony; the tendrils of the plant will climb up the railings which act as a trellis. All varieties of herbs are also wonderful for pots, and they can be conveniently placed as close to the kitchen door as possible.

Seeds and sprouts

Growing seeds and beans indoors is an alternative for anyone with very restricted mobility who cannot maintain a garden plot or pots. Mustard or cress seeds, available in sachets from nurseries, can be grown indoors in a sunny position on wet cotton wool. Avocado seeds placed on the top of a jar of water will sprout readily—first the roots will appear, followed by the stem and leaves. The plant can be potted up when strong enough and in time planted out in the garden, where it will grow and eventually bear fruit (if you live in the warm—temperate to tropical—areas of Australia).

Beans, either soya or mung, alfalfa or lentil, will sprout easily. Buy the seeds from a health food store with the guarantee that they are unpolluted and free from pesticides. Soak the seeds for about 12 hours, then drain off the dirty water. Place the seeds in a large, clean, jar and cover the jar with fine net or a piece of stocking. Change the water twice each day. In three days the seeds will sprout. The food value of sprouts is unsurpassed. Whenever the sprouts and roots have reached the desired length they can be eaten.

Violas

WINDOW BOXES

Window boxes are a good way of enjoying plants and having them within easy reach. Flowers or plants with interesting leaves can be grown to brighten a room, and herbs can be grown to add flavour and interest to the kitchen (see the **Herbs** section [p 39] for more ideas).

Many other plants can be planted in pots: perfumed shrubs such as Gardenias; plants with wonderful flowers such as Hydrangeas, Daisies, Pelargonium, or Fuchsias, and don't forget those with

foliage which make a noise in light breeze such as bamboo. The list for container planting is endless. It is simply a matter of personal preference, a little imagination and placing the plant in conditions which are suited to it.

HANGING BASKETS

Hanging baskets will accommodate any plant that will grow in a pot, but for decorative purposes trailing plants are best. Ivy-Leafed Geraniums are perfect specimens for baskets in a sunny position, and provide a brilliant display. They come

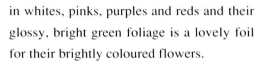

in whites, pinks, purples and reds and their glossy, bright green foliage is a lovely foil for their brightly coloured flowers.

If you live in a tropical climate or have a warm sheltered position in a temperate coastal area, use Bougainvillea 'Rosenka' in a hanging basket. It is one of the smaller growers, ideally suited to container growing and has lovely apricot-coloured flowers.

Ferns also adapt well to hanging baskets, and are suited to fully shaded positions or dappled light. Keep them moist at all times.

Hanging baskets and pot specimens dry out much quicker than those in the garden, so it is crucial to check whether the plant needs moisture. One way to determine whether the plant needs water is to place your index finger into the potting mix: if it is dry to the knuckle it needs water.

A long-handled hose or 'watering wand' will make watering hanging baskets much easier if you are in a wheelchair. Alternatively, if your pots and hanging baskets are under a pergola, the system of black hosing now available at nurseries can be attached to the pergola and the nozzles fitted directly above your baskets. This makes watering them as simple as turning on your tap.

Hanging baskets can be made more accessible by attaching them to a pulley system. You can lower them to check on moisture levels in the potting mix, water them if necessary, then raise them again by pulling the rope.

FUNCTIONAL USE OF FOLIAGE

Plant texture can be used not only for the pleasure of touch, it can also define boundaries, mark positions and create limits to pathways and walkways: particularly useful for people with some type of visual impairment.

Paths and walkways can be created by forming side plantings of low-growing shrubs with distinctive foliage. One example of a suitable plant would be *Grevillea juniperina*. Ensure that the specimens you choose are not too prickly. Choose a plant distinctive enough to indicate the presence of a boundary without resorting to something dangerous.

To mark a position in a garden, select a shrub which grows to about 1.5 or 2 m tall, with distinctive foliage. Once again, the Grevilleas spring to mind. Boundaries can be defined by planting textured hedges. If your garden has been divided into sections

—perhaps lawn, vegetable patch and flower garden—hedges can be planted to define and divide these sections. Use a dense, small-leafed, tightly foliaged plant such as English Box or Box-leafed Honeysuckle. Once established, these boundaries will act as tactile guides leading from one area of the garden to another. Hedges require a lot of maintaining, but once they have been established aim to keep them clipped to about hip level to act as a guide.

CARRY BAG

A material carry bag for tools and weeds is most useful. It is strong, and the material has a plastic lining to help protect it so that the bag will last longer. It can be laid out flat to be used, and the large handles allow it to be picked up easily, scooping up the weeds and taking them away.

Carry bag

THE STORY OF PETER MEAGHER AND HIS NO DIG GARDEN

You cannot give happiness to others without getting some yourself.

Peter is physically spastic, well educated, and always interested in learning and seeking new experiences. Peter married a very loving and caring Janet, and they made their home at Engadine, a suburb of Sydney. Later Janet and Peter were blessed with a bright and healthy son, Timothy.

Unfortunately, the land surrounding their home was impossible to dig and their dream of having a garden seemed to finish. However, on telling their disappointment to friends, one said: 'Why not try Esther Deans' idea of making gardens without digging?' This photo shows the amazing results they achieved by doing so.

I learned about Peter Meagher and his wonderful garden through an article written about him in a local newspaper. The story told of Peter's garden, which had been made on very poor soil that was impossible to dig because of heavy clay and bad drainage. From this terrible start Peter has produced a beautiful garden with award-winning flowers and vegetables.

Peter Meagher's first No Dig garden

The awards, which included eighty-five first, second and champion places, tell an incredible story. Not only did he transform an empty backyard, he grew various plants in pots and sold many at local shows and fetes, under the banner 'Peter's plants', which became well known because they always grew.

Peter made sure the plants were growing in good soil.

Peter also had some other outside interests, besides being employed by the Sydney County Council. He accepted the position of Treasurer of the Geranium Society, and is a member of the Engadine Lawn Bowling Club. Peter is a very happy family man, interested in life to a great degree.

It was rewarding to visit Peter's garden, and to know his wife Janet and son Timothy, and to see for myself what has happened to an empty backyard. Eventually, Don Burke on his TV show 'Burke's Backyard' showed to all people just how people with a disability can make a garden.

This book has shown the wonderful achievements of people of all ages with disabilities.

FROM GARDEN TO KITCHEN

HONEY-GLAZED CARROTS WITH MINT

6 medium-sized carrots, halved　　　　*2 dessertspoons honey*

2 dessertspoons butter　　　　*½ teaspoon vegetable salt*

½ teaspoon dry mint leaves

Wash carrots thoroughly and halve. Cook in the smallest possible amount of water until tender and allow to drain. Melt butter in pan. Stir in mint leaves and let stand for a few minutes. Blend in honey and vegetable salt. Bring to boil. Add carrots and simmer a few minutes until glazed.

Serves 4

LEMON-HERB BUTTER

½ cup soft butter or margarine　　　　*1 teaspoon snipped parsley*

1 tablespoon grated lemon rind　　　　*½ teaspoon snipped chives*

½ teaspoon dried basil

Work the butter in a small dish until creamy. Add lemon rind and herbs and refrigerate for several hours before use. Use it to spread on hot cooked vegetables.

CASSEROLE COOKING

You can casserole waterlessly by grating root vegetables and slicing or chopping the more succulent types. If you place a lettuce leaf on the bottom of the casserole you will need very little water. Fill the casserole to the top, cover tightly and then bake in a moderate oven.

PUMPKIN PIE

2 eggs

½ cup brown sugar

½ cup milk

1 cup mashed cooked pumpkin

1 teaspoon mixed spice

pinch salt

some blanched almonds

Use normal ingredients for standard piecrust pastry.

Line a 23 cm pie plate with pastry. Beat the eggs, adding sugar and milk, then the mashed pumpkin, spice and salt. Mix thoroughly and put into pastry case. Arrange the almonds on top in a decorative pattern and bake in a moderate oven for about 45 minutes. Allow to cool and serve topped with a little cream. The basic method for cooking pumpkin is to remove the skin and seeds and cut into conveniently sized pieces.

SAUTÉED EGGPLANT

1 medium-sized onion, diced

vegetable oil

vegetable salt

1 tablespoon milk

2 medium-sized tomatoes, skinned and finely chopped

2 medium-sized eggplants

Fry the diced onion in a little oil. Add vegetable salt to taste, milk and tomatoes. Cook for about ten minutes. Slice eggplants into thickish rounds and cook in oil until they are golden brown in colour. Pour the sauce over them. Cover with a lid and cook until soft.

Serves 4

Herb teas are so refreshing when the herbs are picked
from your garden

This book cannot be finished without telling this beautiful story.

A dear lady who spent 20 years of her life in an iron lung as a result of polio had decided that she would like to do something to show the gratitude she felt for all the help received over the years. She asked all her visitors and helpers to save their used stamps so that the money from the sale of the stamps could be given to charity.

The request passed from person to person with Sunday School children being asked to collect used stamps from their parents. Office workers and people working in clubs and shops also joined in the collection. The result was overwhelming.

Stamps arrived by the bagful. Another patient at the hospital, who spent her days in a wheelchair, was able to trim the stamps and prepare them for sale. Stamp saving has now become an integral part of therapy there.

❖ ❖ ❖

Because of all the wonderful stories you have read and the photos you have seen, I am sure you will agree words like 'handicapped' and 'disabled' do not apply. Perhaps we should say 'handicapable'.

I dedicate this book to all handicapable people, with many blessings.

Thanks for sharing,
Happy gardening
Esther Deans.

INDEX

This book is not intended to be comprehensive, but rather indicates popular plants, and those which it may be difficult to track down. Scientific names are provided for the more unusual plants.